Q&A Kids

ELECTRICITY

AMY CHAPMAN
ANGELIKA SCUDAMORE

WINDMILL BOOKS

Published in 2026 by Windmill Books,
an Imprint of Rosen Publishing
2544 Clinton St.
Buffalo, NY 14224

First published in Great Britain in 2026
by Wayland

Editor: Sarah Peutrill
Designer: Lisa Peacock

Some of the text in this book was
first published in Fact Cat: Electricity
by Izzi Howell

Cataloging-in-Publication Data

Names: Chapman, Amy, author. | Scudamore, Angelika, illustrator.
Title: Electricity / Amy Chapman, illustrated by Angelika Scudamore.
Description: Buffalo, NY : Windmill Books, 2026. | Series: Q & A kids | Includes glossary and index.
Identifiers: ISBN 9781725396135 (pbk.) | ISBN 9781725396142 (library bound) | ISBN 9781725396159 (ebook)
Subjects: LCSH: Electricity--Juvenile literature.
Classification: LCC QC527.2 C437 2026 | DDC 537--dc23

Printed in the United States of America

CPSIA Compliance Information: Batch #CSWM26
For Further Information contact Rosen Publishing
at 1-800-237-9932

CONTENTS

Can you spot me in this book? There are 13 to find, not counting this one.

WHAT IS ELECTRICITY?

Q. What is electricity?

A. Electricity is a type of energy. We use electricity to power many objects in our homes, such as computers, televisions, and lights.

We use electricity to power large machines, such as electric trains.

Electricity travels very fast. It can move almost 10 million feet (3 million m) in one second!

FIND IT

How many things powered by electricity can you find in the picture?

NATURAL OR HUMAN-MADE?

Q. Where does electricity come from?

A. Electricity can be made by people or it can be found already in nature.

Electrical appliances are powered by current electricity. This is a type of electricity that we make. It can move along wires from one place to another.

Lightning is a type of natural electricity called static electricity (see page 26). The static electricity stays up in the clouds until it shoots down to the ground as lightning.

We also find electricity in animals! Find out more on page 28.

SORT IT

Can you sort the types of electricity in the pictures into natural or man-made?

A.

B.

C.

D.

E.

F.

MAKING ELECTRICITY

Q. How do we make electricity?

A. Most electricity is produced using huge machines in power stations.

To make electricity, the power station first burns a fuel, such as coal. They use the heat to boil water, which makes steam. Then, the steam makes a turbine wheel spin around. Finally, the spinning turbine powers a generator, which produces electricity.

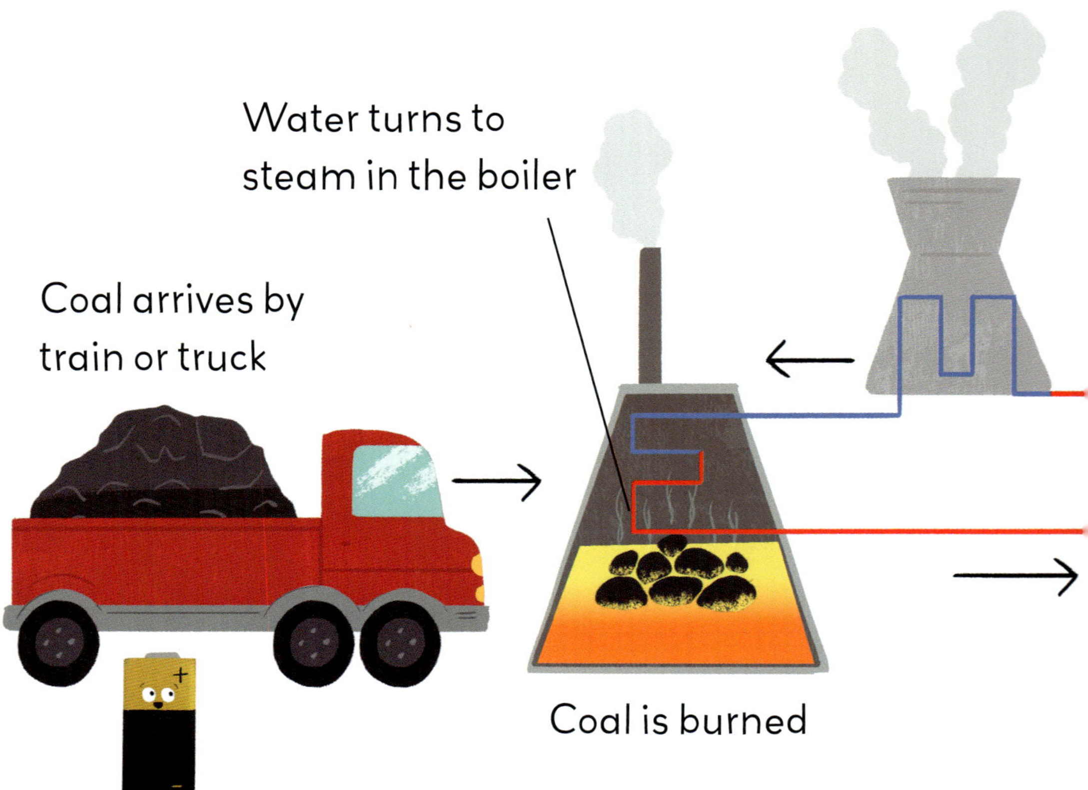

Electricity travels along power lines to where it is needed. The electricity in these wires is dangerous and very strong. Metal towers hold up the wires so that they are far from the ground.

FOLLOW IT

Follow the diagram to see how electricity is made in power stations.

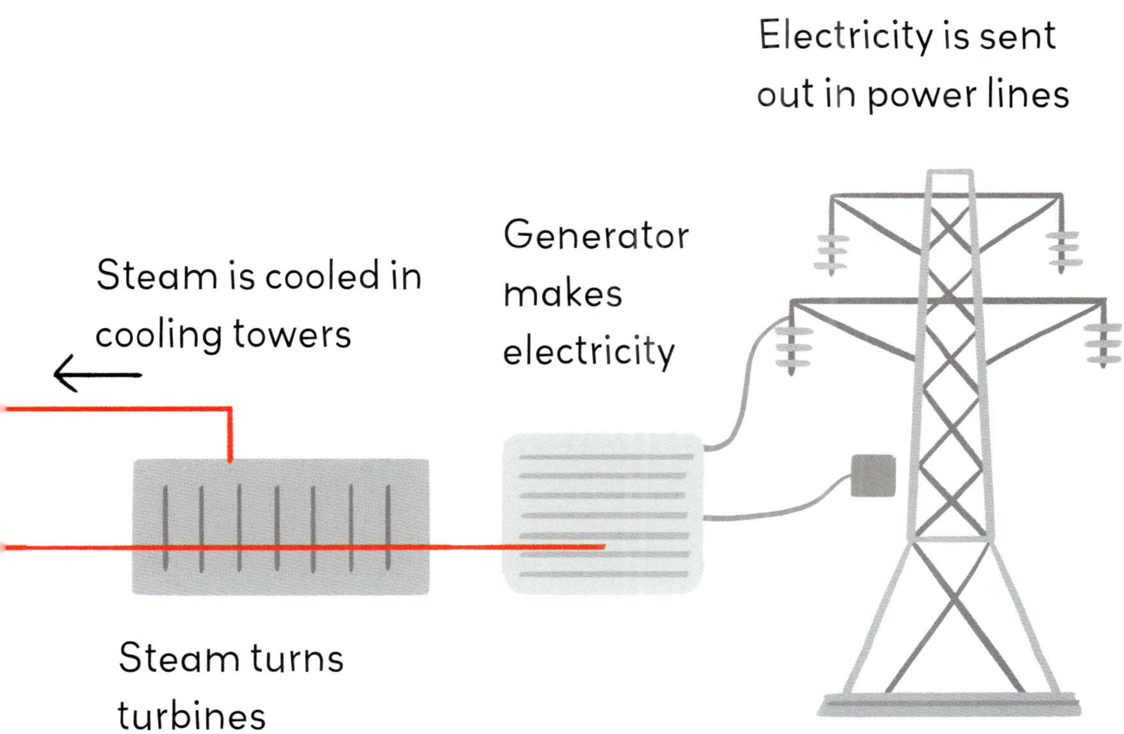

FLOWING ALONG

Q. Where does the electricity go?

A. From the power station, electricity flows through large lines, which carry it to substations. Finally, distribution lines carry electricity from substations to homes, businesses, and schools.

At the power station, after electricity has been made, the leftover steam is placed in large towers to cool down. Some of it escapes into the air.

Power stations that burn fuel are bad for the environment. This is because burning fuel makes a gas called carbon dioxide, which can damage the Earth.

THINK ABOUT IT

There are lampposts on these streets. What are they for?

SOLAR POWER

Q. Are there other ways to make electricity, apart from coal?

A. Yes, we can also make electricity from other things including sunlight, wind, and water.

It is better for the environment to make electricity in these ways. Some people use solar panels to make electricity to use in their house. Solar panels contain a material that makes electricity when the Sun shines on it.

THINK ABOUT IT

Roofs are a good place to put solar panels. Why do you think this is?

WIND AND WATER POWER

Q. How can you make electricity from the wind?

A. Generating electricity from wind or water is similar to generating electricity in a power station. Instead of using steam to push the turbine, the movement of wind or water makes the turbine spin.

Wind turbines are often placed along the coast or out at sea, where there is a lot of wind.

People have made energy from wind and water for hundreds of years. In the past, people used windmills and watermills to grind flour and power simple machines.

FIND OUT

Dams are one way to make electricity from water. Find out if there are any dams where you live.

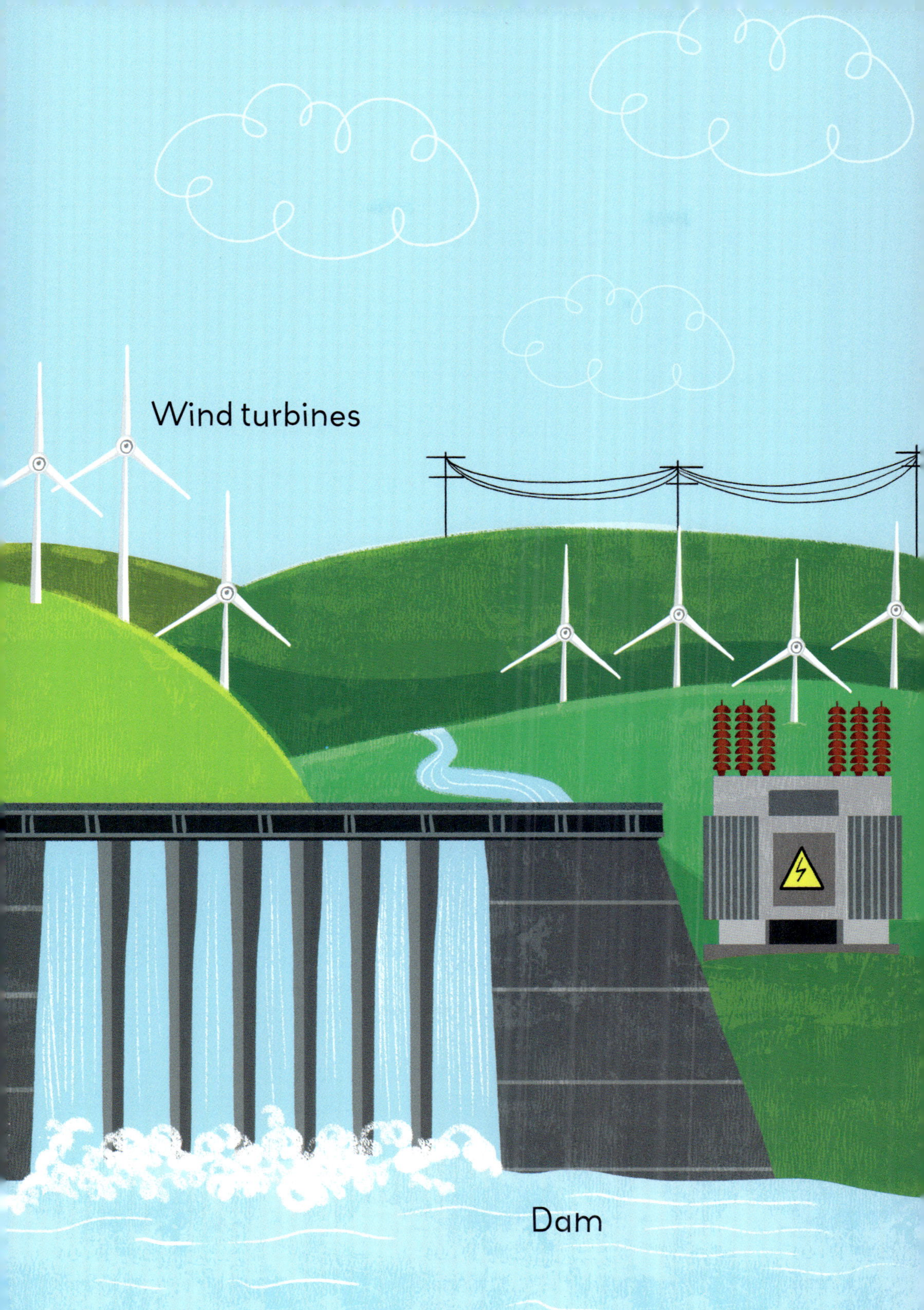
Wind turbines
Dam

BATTERIES

Q. How do we keep electricity ready for when we need it?

A. We can store electricity in a battery. Batteries have two sides – the positive side and the negative side. They have to be placed the right way around.

Inside all batteries, there are chemicals that make electricity. Eventually, batteries stop working when all of the chemicals inside them have been used up.

When batteries stop working, it is important to never throw them away in a trash can. Batteries should be taken to be recycled so the chemicals inside can be used again.

FIND IT

Which toys in the picture run on batteries? Which don't need batteries?

A.
B.
C.
D.
E.
F.
G.
H.
I.
J.

CIRCUITS

Q. I've got wires, a battery, and a bulb, but nothing is happening. Why not?

A. You need to make a circuit. A circuit is a path around which electricity can travel. In a circuit, there are always wires and a power source, such as a battery. You can also add other parts, such as buzzers or bulbs.

In the circuit in the picture, electricity comes out of the battery. It flows through the wires and back into the battery. The bulb is giving out light because it is powered by the battery.

THINK ABOUT IT

If you added another lamp to this circuit, the electricity from the battery would be split between the two lamps. Both lamps would give out less light. What would happen if you added another battery?

Bulb
Battery
Wire

SWITCHES

Q. What does a switch do?

A. In a circuit, electricity only flows if a switch is closed and the circuit is complete, with no gaps. If the switch is open, no electricity will flow.

Most electrical appliances have switches. Switches stop and start the flow of electricity through a circuit.

Switching off lights when you leave a room helps to save electricity. It also saves money, as you have to pay to use electricity.

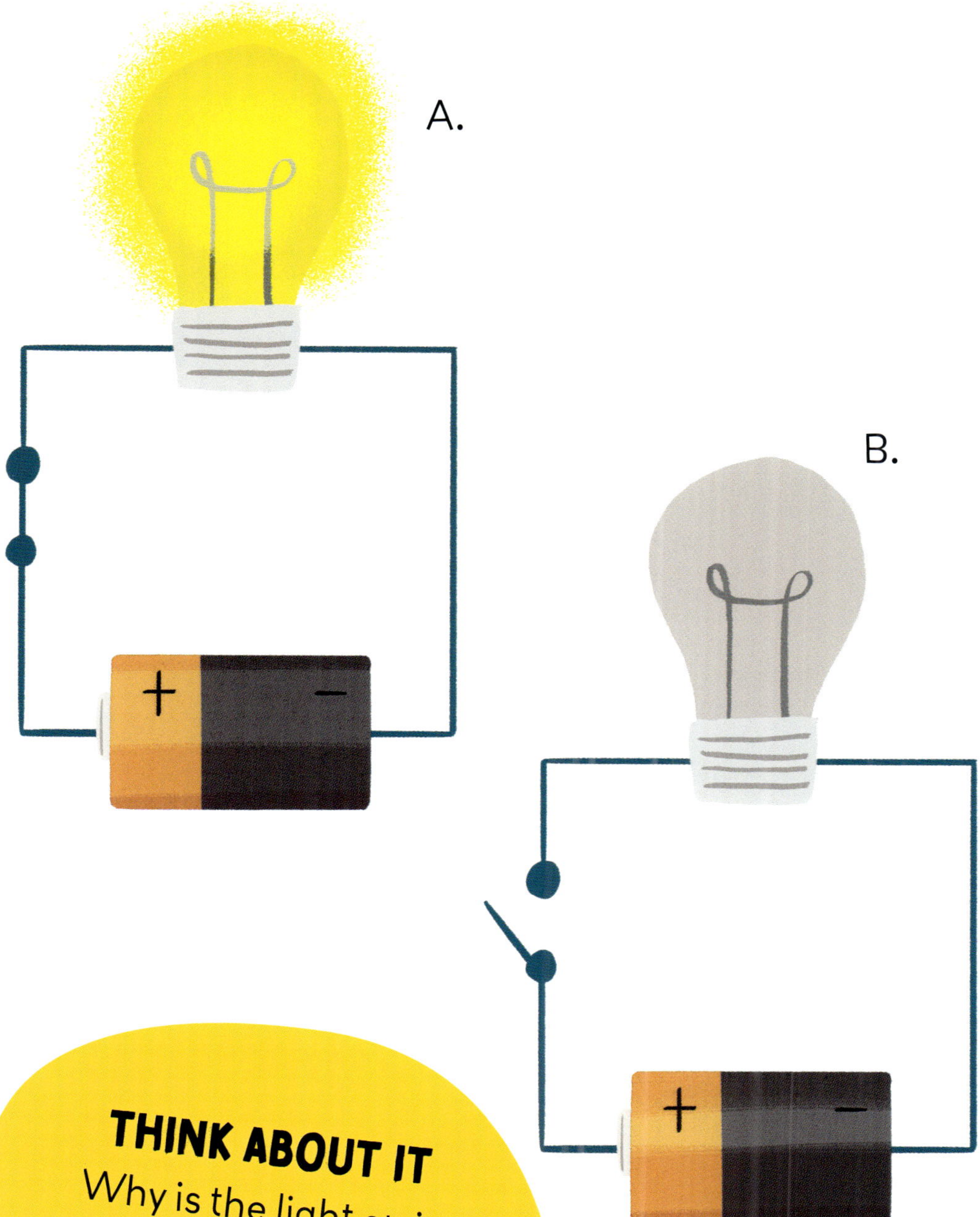

THINK ABOUT IT
Why is the light on in circuit A but off in B?

CONDUCTORS AND INSULATORS

Q. What are electric wires made from?

A. The wires in a circuit have to conduct electricity. Electrical conductors are materials that let electricity pass through them. Most metals are electrical conductors. Wires are usually made from a metal called copper.

Electrical insulators do not let electricity pass through them. Some examples of electrical insulators are wood, plastic, and glass. Insulators are important in a circuit, as they stop electricity from escaping.

The outside of electrical wires and plugs are covered with plastic so that they are safe to hold.

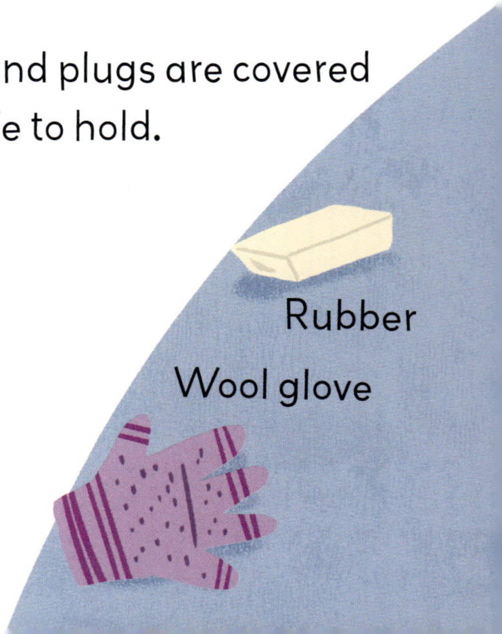

SORT IT

Ben has to sort these objects into electrical conductors and insulators. Can you help?

ELECTRICAL SAFETY

Q. Why do I have to be careful around electricity?

A. Electricity is useful, but it can also be very dangerous. A small amount of electricity can give you a painful electric shock. A lot of electricity can kill you.

Never touch any outdoor electrical switches or wires.

Electricity can pass through water. This is why it is very dangerous to get an electrical appliance wet or to touch one with wet hands.

Electricity can conduct through different materials, so you should never put anything other than a plug inside an electric socket. The electricity might travel through the object into your body.

THINK ABOUT IT

Here are four times when you would need to be aware. Think about why in each case.

A.

B.

C.

D.

STATIC ELECTRICITY

Q. What does static electricity do?

A. Static electricity can make things stick together. For example, if you rub a balloon on your hair, it creates static electricity that will make the balloon stick to a wall.

You can bend water with static electricity. If you rub a comb through your hair and then hold the comb next to a running tap, the stream of water will bend.

Static electricity can also sometimes give you a tiny little shock.

TRY IT

Static electricity can make your hair stand on end. Try rubbing a balloon on your hair and then hold the balloon near your head.

ELECTRIC ANIMALS

Q. Do animals, like electric eels, really contain electricity?

A. Yes, all animals, including humans, make small amounts of electricity. This electricity sends signals around our body, telling it what to do.

Sharks can sense the electricity in other animals. This helps them to find fish to eat.

FIND OUT

Which body part helps a honeybee make electricity?

Some animals can make large amounts of electricity. The electric eel lives in rivers in the rainforests of South America. They can send out electricity to hurt and kill their prey. An electric eel can create an electric shock that is several times stronger than the electricity in a socket.

QUIZ

1. Most electricity is made in power stations. True or not true?

a) true

b) not true

2. Which of these parts supplies electricity in a circuit?

a) wire

b) battery

c) lamp

3. If a switch is open, electricity flows through the circuit. True or not true?

a) true

b) not true

4. Which material conducts electricity?

a) copper

b) wood

c) plastic

5. It is dangerous to fly kites near overhead wires. True or not true?

a) true

b) not true

6. Which animal senses electricity?

a) rabbit

b) chicken

c) shark

Quiz answers

1. a – true
2. b – battery
3. b – not true (electricity only flows through a complete circuit with a closed switch)
4. a – copper
5. a – true
6. c – shark

GLOSSARY

boil when a liquid is boiled, it reaches a temperature when it makes bubbles and steam

buzzer an electrical device that makes a sound

carbon dioxide a gas that is made when fuel is burned that is bad for the environment

coal a hard black substance that can be burned

conductor something that lets electricity pass through

current electricity electricity that can move along wires from one place to another

electric shock a sudden painful feeling that you get when electricity passes through your body

environment the air, water, and land where living things live

fuel something that is burned to make heat or power

gas something that is neither a solid nor a liquid, such as air

generator a machine that makes electricity

insulator something that does not let electricity pass through

power to supply energy to a machine and make it work

power station a factory where electricity is made

prey an animal that is hunted and killed by another animal

sense to feel or experience something

socket the place in the wall where you can connect a cable to the electrical supply

solar panel a machine that turns light from the Sun into electricity

static electricity electricity that stays in one place

steam gas made when water boils

turbine a large machine that makes electricity by turning a wheel

INDEX

SOME ANSWERS

p. 4–5 Seven: radio, lamp, computer, printer, TV, flashlight, and remote-controlled car.
p. 6–7 Natural electricity: B, C and E. Man-made electricity: A, D and F.
p. 10 Streetlamps help people and cars on busy streets to see well at night.
p. 13 A roof usually gets a lot of sunlight making it a good place for solar panels.
p. 16–17 Toys that need batteries: A, E and I. Toys that don't need batteries: B, C, D, F, G, H and J.
p. 19 If you add another battery, both lamps will give out bright light.
p. 21 In A. the switch is closed, completing the circuit and allowing electricity to reach the bulb. In B. the open switch stops this from happening.